"In The Beginning" Chronologically Speaking Bible Supports Richard Dawkins

Copyright 2016 Clayton B Carlson
Published by First Page Solutions

ISBN-10: 198822604X
ISBN-13: 978-1988226040

License Notes

Table of Contents

CHAPTER 1

Many books and stories don't start at the beginning. They will start part way through the story or sometimes at the end of it to help give some dramatic flair. Movies may use the same technique in order to create intrigue or to give a new perspective to a caricature. The Star Wars movie franchise comes to mind. The first movie started further along in the story, not until later in the series are we given the true beginning revealing a soft side to the dreaded Darth Vader and filling in lingering questions we may have had about the first movies in the series.

It seems to me God has used this technique in the bible. He tells us that we need to study his word and take a little from here and a precept from there. Here a little and there a little, to help reveal all of the wisdom's he has for us.

When we look at the bible and want to start at the very beginning chronologically speaking, we shouldn't start in the book of Genesis. We should rather look for references that happened at the earliest times recorded in the bible. This would be in John were we are told the word was with God, and that the word was God.

John 1:1-3 (KJV)
1 In the beginning was the Word, and the Word was with God, and the Word was God.
2 The same was in the beginning with God.
3 All things were made by him; and without him was not anything made that was made.

These verses put us in a time when we are only told of the existence of God. This is before any creating had started, a time before the angelic beings, a time God was planning the end of things before the beginning had started. For God knows the end to the beginning, he tells us in:

Isaiah 46:10 (KJV)
10 Declaring the end from the beginning, and from ancient times the things that are not yet done, saying, My counsel shall stand, and I will do all my pleasure: He has it planned out. God was the first reverse engineer.

The next glimpse we get into the distant past is when the angels sang for joy over the beauty of the new world God had just created.

Job 38:4-7 (KJV)

4 Where wast thou when I laid the foundations of the earth? declare, if thou hast understanding.
5 Who hath laid the measures thereof, if thou knowest? or who hath stretched the line upon it?
6 Whereupon are the foundations thereof fastened? or who laid the corner stone thereof;
7 When the morning stars sang together, and all the sons of God shouted for joy?

In our imagination we can perhaps see the splendour of the earth as seen from space. A shining blue orb on a backdrop of black with tiny sparkles of light. Or maybe you imagine one of the many vistas of grandeur that our planet has to offer. Perhaps you are awed buy one of the mysteries the word has hidden in its secret places, glimpsed at by only a select few. Whatever our imaginations conjure up, it is clear the angels thought it was very spectacular as they sang with joy from its beauty.

CHAPTER 2

Then history takes on a darker more sinister tone. Sin has made its way into God's Kingdom and it starts with his most beautiful creation.

Ezekiel 28:12-17 (KJV)
12 Son of man, take up a lamentation upon the king of Tyrus, and say unto him, Thus saith the Lord God; Thou sealest up the sum, full of wisdom, and perfect in beauty.
13 Thou hast been in Eden the garden of God; every precious stone was thy covering, the sardius, topaz, and the diamond, the beryl, the onyx, and the jasper, the sapphire, the emerald, and the carbuncle, and gold: the workmanship of thy tabrets and of thy pipes was prepared in thee in the day that thou wast created.
14 Thou art the anointed cherub that covereth; and I have set thee so: thou wast upon the holy mountain of God; thou hast walked up and down in the midst of the stones of fire.
15 Thou wast perfect in thy ways from the day that thou wast created, till iniquity was found in thee.

16 By the multitude of thy merchandise they have filled the midst of thee with violence, and thou hast sinned: therefore I will cast thee as profane out of the mountain of God: and I will destroy thee, O covering cherub, from the midst of the stones of fire.
17 Thine heart was lifted up because of thy beauty, thou hast corrupted thy wisdom by reason of thy brightness: I will cast thee to the ground, I will lay thee before kings, that they may behold thee.

The sin quickly spreads and infects one third of God's angels.

Revelation 12:4 (KJV)
4 And his tail drew the third part of the stars of heaven, and did cast them to the earth: and the dragon stood before the woman which was ready to be delivered, for to devour her child as soon as it was born.

In order to stamp out the sin a fierce battle rages between the angels. Most stay loyal to their creator but some rebel against God and side with Satan. The rebels are cast out of heaven and into the earth along with Satan.

Revelation 12:7-9 (KJV)

7 And there was war in heaven: Michael and his angels fought against the dragon; and the dragon fought and his angels,

8 And prevailed not; neither was their place found any more in heaven.

9 And the great dragon was cast out, that old serpent, called the Devil, and Satan, which deceiveth the whole world: he was cast out into the earth, and his angels were cast out with him.

We are given the reason for the war in the heavens, the source of Lucifer's sin. Pride led Lucifer to reject God and try to depose him from his throne. He now awaits his pending doom.

Isaiah 14:12-15 (KJV)

12 How art thou fallen from heaven, O Lucifer, son of the morning! how art thou cut down to the ground, which didst weaken the nations!

13 For thou hast said in thine heart, I will ascend into heaven, I will exalt my throne above the stars of God: I will sit also upon the mount of the congregation, in the sides of the north:

14 I will ascend above the heights of the clouds; I will be like the most High.

15 Yet thou shalt be brought down to hell, to the sides of the pit.

Jesus recounts to his disciples how he saw Satan's fall from grace.

Luke 10:17-18 (KJV)
17 And the seventy returned again with joy, saying, Lord, even the devils are subject unto us through thy name.
18 And he said unto them, I beheld Satan as lightning fall from heaven.

CHAPTER 3

Now we come to the account of Genesis. Is this the beginning of time in the bible as some claim? It may be, but that is a question we each should answer for ourselves. It may the kind of question where our answer will change after thoughtful consideration of different points of view. Over time we may never be fully convinced either way as we weigh all of the evidence, or new evidence may come up to sway our thinking the other way. It is a peripheral topic of Christianity after all. Our faith should be built on nothing less than Jesus Christ. He is the rock we need to cling to, he alone has the power to save. As we read in:

Genesis 1:1 (KJV), In the beginning God created the heaven and the earth.

We see God as the creator. In this first verse there is no reference given as to when he did this creating. It could have been much earlier, or he could have created it right then.

Verses 2-5 covers the first day or period of time. God separates the light and darkness. He would have had to create the universe now at this time for it to all happen on the first day. If you take the point of view there was a time gap between the first and second verse, then he could have started the universe building process at some time previously. We are told by astronomers the universe is continuing to expand and grow. New stars and solar systems are being created now as you read this. Science is continuing to make new discoveries about the mysterious universe as our technology develops.

The building and growing of the universe is not stagnant. It wasn't finished on that first day. God's creation has continued to grow and change here on the earth as well as the universe. Looking at it this way God had not finished creation, but had just started the process in verse one. However taking the audience into account he didn't talk beyond their understanding, but conveyed the basic message so all could understand.

2 And the earth was without form, and void; and darkness was upon the face of the deep. And the Spirit of God moved upon the face of the waters. 3 And God said, Let there be light: and there was light.

4 And God saw the light, that it was good: and God divided the light from the darkness.
5 And God called the light Day, and the darkness he called Night. And the evening and the morning were the first day.

Verses 6-8 God divides the waters with heaven or atmosphere.

6 And God said, Let there be a firmament in the midst of the waters, and let it divide the waters from the waters.
7 And God made the firmament, and divided the waters which were under the firmament from the waters which were above the firmament: and it was so.
8 And God called the firmament Heaven. And the evening and the morning were the second day.

Verses 9-13 we see God making dry land, seas and the flora of the earth.

9 And God said, Let the waters under the heaven be gathered together unto one place, and let the dry land appear: and it was so.
10 And God called the dry land Earth; and the gathering together of the waters called he Seas: and God saw that it was good.

11 And God said, Let the earth bring forth grass, the herb yielding seed, and the fruit tree yielding fruit after his kind, whose seed is in itself, upon the earth: and it was so.

12 And the earth brought forth grass, and herb yielding seed after his kind, and the tree yielding fruit, whose seed was in itself, after his kind: and God saw that it was good.

13 And the evening and the morning were the third day.

Verses 14-19 tells us it is now that the sun, moon, and stars are created. I find it strange they wouldn't have been made on the first day with the rest of the universe. Where would the light have come from on the first day if the sun wasn't made until now? I know God can make it work if he wants to step outside of the physical systems he has set up. However this account of creation doesn't seem to work inside those physical limitations.

Was day one more of a miracle than we had thought? Did he make light appear miraculously? Could it be that these stories of creation are from an earthly vantage point looking up? If you have ever been in a bad storm it can be hard to tell day from night. But as the sky's clear you can make out the sun. The clearer the sky becomes the more that is revealed from a terrestrial point of view. Thinking of it in this light makes a person less dogmatic and stringent on how God created things. Taking the scriptures literally may lead to some confusion.

14 And God said, Let there be lights in the firmament of the heaven to divide the day from the night; and let them be for signs, and for seasons, and for days, and years:
15 And let them be for lights in the firmament of the heaven to give light upon the earth: and it was so.
16 And God made two great lights; the greater light to rule the day, and the lesser light to rule the night: he made the stars also.
17 And God set them in the firmament of the heaven to give light upon the earth,
18 And to rule over the day and over the night, and to divide the light from the darkness: and God saw that it was good.
19 And the evening and the morning were the fourth day.

Verses 20-23 has God creating sea creatures and birds.

20 And God said, Let the waters bring forth abundantly the moving creature that hath life, and fowl that may fly above the earth in the open firmament of heaven.

21 And God created great whales, and every living creature that moveth, which the waters brought forth abundantly, after their kind, and every winged fowl after his kind: and God saw that it was good.
22 And God blessed them, saying, Be fruitful, and multiply, and fill the waters in the seas, and let fowl multiply in the earth.
23 And the evening and the morning were the fifth day.

The section from verse 24-31 covers all land creatures including man and woman.

24 And God said, Let the earth bring forth the living creature after his kind, cattle, and creeping thing, and beast of the earth after his kind: and it was so.
25 And God made the beast of the earth after his kind, and cattle after their kind, and everything that creepeth upon the earth after his kind: and God saw that it was good.
26 And God said, Let us make man in our image, after our likeness: and let them have dominion over the fish of the sea, and over the fowl of the air, and over the cattle, and over all the earth, and over every creeping thing that creepeth upon the earth.
27 So God created man in his own image, in the image of God created he him; male and female created he them.

28 And God blessed them, and God said unto them, Be fruitful, and multiply, and replenish the earth, and subdue it: and have dominion over the fish of the sea, and over the fowl of the air, and over every living thing that moveth upon the earth.

29 And God said, Behold, I have given you every herb bearing seed, which is upon the face of all the earth, and every tree, in the which is the fruit of a tree yielding seed; to you it shall be for meat.

30 And to every beast of the earth, and to every fowl of the air, and to everything that creepeth upon the earth, wherein there is life, I have given every green herb for meat: and it was so.

31 And God saw everything that he had made, and, behold, it was very good. And the evening and the morning were the sixth day.

Finally God rests after having created all things.

Genesis 2:1-4 (KJV)

1 Thus the heavens and the earth were finished, and all the host of them.

2 And on the seventh day God ended his work which he had made; and he rested on the seventh day from all his work which he had made.

3 And God blessed the seventh day, and sanctified it: because that in it he had rested from all his work which God created and made.

4 These are the generations of the heavens and of the earth when they were created, in the day that the Lord God made the earth and the heavens,

CHAPTER 4

I believe the point to the creation account we have gone through in Genesis is to give humanity a story that can be easily passed down from generation to generation. The Bible is not intended to be a scientific text book. Rather it delivers principles on how we should relate to God and each other. Principles and directions on the essential truths of how we may understand our heavenly father, as well as how to receive the gifts of adoption and eternal life. These are the truths that are vital to understand. The peripheral things don't give life. They may help us live life with a better understanding of our heavenly father but they are by definition peripheral to the essential things of life.

Some people say to me "why do you bother spending your time and energy writing on topics few people agree with you on. Your view point is held by only a few people on the margins of Christianity". To these people I can only say that if looking at the scriptures from this vantage point helps to bring one lost lamb back to the fold of faith in their creator, then I have not wasted my time.

Some studies have shown that forty percent of the young adults from a Christian background turn from their faith after entering post-secondary education. Some speculate it is because of the evolutionary theory and scientific models that are taught there. If this perspective helps one of them to see that God can be the creator of all things, while still looking through the lens of science, in conjunction with the biblical record and coming out with faith in their loving father stronger, then this is time well spent.

Science and biblical studies do not have to be mutually exclusive. Our understanding and interpretation of some scriptures may have to be adjusted, but God wrote his word to be a living record to mankind throughout the ages. Not a book that would get stale and out of date, but rather one that would be a blessing to all generations.

If this vantage point of the scriptures helps someone who has no hope for their future. Someone that sees the life lived with nothing that will last at the end, but the possibility of their gene pool being carried on, as futile and hollow. Then looking at the scriptures not as a scientific text book, but as a relevant guide for their lives that holds great promise for the future, could introduce them to faith. If these thoughts can help them see God and the future he has for them, it is worth it.

I know people who specifically reject Christianity because of the teaching that the world can be no more than seven thousand years old. Reading the scriptures on this peripheral topic showing creation week to be actually re-creation week can give them options they may never have heard expressed before.

To those Christians that say I am distorting the truth of God's inspired word I say, "relax a bit" this is after all a peripheral subject. I think we need to make room for science in our biblical doctrines. To say that there is no possibility what so ever that creation as recorded in Gen.1 was a re-creation, is dictatorial and high handed.

Some will say to me, to think that it could be an account of re-creation goes against the orthodoxy of most Christian denominations, and that we need to keep the faith as it was handed down to us lest we drift from God. Do these arguments stand the test of history? Let's go back five hundred years in church history and see.

CHAPTER 5

Galileo's dispute with the ruling church was over the time tested biblically proven belief that said the world did not move and that it was the centre of the universe. The scriptures used to support this doctrine were.

Psalm 93:1 (KJV)
The Lord reigneth, he is clothed with majesty; the Lord is clothed with strength, wherewith he hath girded himself: the world also is stablished, that it cannot be moved.

Psalm 96:10 (KJV)
Say among the heathen that the Lord reigneth: the world also shall be established that it shall not be moved: he shall judge the people righteously.

1 Chronicles 16:30 (KJV)
Fear before him, all the earth: the world also shall be stable, that it be not moved.

Psalm 104:5 (KJV)
Who laid the foundations of the earth, that it should not be removed for ever.

Ecclesiastes 1:5 (KJV)
The sun also ariseth, and the sun goeth down, and hasteth to his place where he arose.

Would the supporters of the creation week being the literal reading of Gen.1 also support the church's belief from five hundred years ago? If not why? It was only changed after being challenged by science. Have the bible verses changed? Has the authority of God been diminished by our understanding of how our solar system works? No, nothing has changed, God is still sovereign, the bible is still his word. The only thing that has changed is our understanding of his word and how we interpret its meaning. To believe in a world older that seven thousand years does not remove God from being the creator of all things.

Genesis 1:1 (KJV) 1 In the beginning God created the heaven and the earth.

God tell us in Genesis that he created all life. How and when he did this creating, may be debatable, but not his role as creator.

CHAPTER 6

Scientists may scoff at the thought of a creator. But when asked about where the matter to go bang came from or how it managed to bang to start with, they don't seem to have many answers. It's almost like they forgo the scientific methods of repeatable proof and take it on faith.

It reminds me of the story of a scientific team that said they could create life. They were so sure of themselves they challenged God to a race to start a life. God shows up to find out the rules for the race and they start explaining how each team can only have one pound of dirt and two cups of clean water. To which God replied "you can make your own dirt and water".

The scientific law of the story is that something can't come from nothing. No matter how creation started it had to have a creator to make even the most basic elements. They didn't come from nothing.

BIBLE SUPPORTS RICHARD DAWKINS

As a Biblist who tries to take all scripture pertaining to a subject into account, I find the Bible agrees with Richard Dawkins assertion that the earth is more than seven thousand years old. Bible scriptures and arguments that do not take the polar opposite position to that of the scientists are seldom given much publicity in the creation versus evolution debate.

Lacking controversy, their value as a marketing tool is limited in our world of salesmanship and hype. It is from the middle ground that we will find the origins of our universe, as well as discover the creative forces that got it all started. Learning from other historical debates as well as reading the Bible through biblist eyes we can find this common ground.

Famous scientist, author and professor Richard Dawkins is well known for his public debates in opposition to creationists. The tone of these debates are normally adversarial, as those engaged in these clashes hold extreme opposite opinions for the age of the universe. If not for the strong disagreements of the participants, these debates wouldn't garner much attention.

As a casual observer of such debates, I had thought Mr. Dawkins was opposed to all creationists. This is why his comment on the CBC Radio show Day Six, Episode 254 which aired on Oct. 9. 2015 caught my attention. Brent Bambery interviewed Richard Dawkins, asking him questions about his recent public statements made on his twitter account, as well as on his new memoir, Brief Candle in the Dark: My Life in Science.

The part of the interview that peaked my interest was when Professor Dawkins made the statement, "that a young earth creationist who believes that the world is only six thousand years old is not necessarily stupid but they are ignorant of the facts." He suggests "that they need to go away and read a book". I found the distinction given to the new earth creationist quite interesting. This distinction highlights the fact that not all creationists have the same beliefs for the process of creation. Similar to the way all scientists may not have the same beliefs for the process of "The Big Bang". As an old earth creationist, I would agree with some of the hypotheses Professor Dawkins puts forward.

As most of us instinctively know, the two philosophical extremes of a subject are not correct and that the truth is usually found somewhere in the middle of those two positions. To help find the middle ground we need only revisit a debate that happened in the early fifteen hundreds.

This debate pitted Christianity, and the scientists of the day against each other. Now with the 20/20 vision of hind sight, Christianity now has no problem agreeing with those early scientific conclusions. In recognizing the now clearly correct scientific conclusions, Christians today realize the beliefs and traditions that shaped their earlier understanding for the workings of our solar system, were wrong. These ancient beliefs had stood for thousands of years, and had taken thousands of years to be developed.

The authority of the Bible featured prominently in the debate then, as it does in the creation debate of today. Christians hold the Bible to be true today, just as they held it to be true in the fifteen hundreds. Perhaps the change needed for today, is the same change that took place back then? This change was not the abandonment of the

Bible as a source of truth, but in the perspective the reader has when reading Bible scriptures. Rather than reading the Bible as a scientific text book that is providing hard facts, Christians of today read the verses used in this old debate now as metaphor, allowing for poetic license to be taken by the scriptures of the Bible.

The debate I am referring to is the debate brought to a head by Galileo. He believed his nightly observations of the celestial bodies through his tubes of leather and glass proved that the earth did indeed move around them. In doing so he was declaring the long standing belief that the world stood still and did not move to be false. This declaration called the authority of the Bible into question, which brought him into sharp dispute with the Christian establishment of the day. The Christian elite relied on a literal understanding for the following Biblical scriptures to support the truth as they read it.

Psalm 93:1 (KJV)
1 The Lord reigneth, he is clothed with majesty; the Lord is clothed with strength, wherewith he hath girded himself: the world also is established, that it cannot be moved.

Psalm 96:10 (KJV)

10 Say among the heathen that the Lord reigneth: the world also shall be established that it shall not be moved: he shall judge the people righteously

1 Chronicles 16:30 (KJV)
30 Fear before him, all the earth: the world also shall be stable, that it be not moved

Psalm 104:5 (KJV)
5 Who laid the foundations of the earth, that it should not be removed for ever.

Ecclesiastes 1:5 (KJV)
5 The sun also ariseth, and the sun goeth down, and hasteth to his place where he arose.

These verses, from a literal perspective, undoubtedly tell us the earth will not move. However from our world of space travel and scientific exploration, Christians today understand them outside of the factual truth the early biblical scholars held them to be. Christians today have no qualms in understanding these verses as metaphor and story, allowing for poetic license.

Holding to the scientific understanding of the solar system's workings, creates no crises of faith in the authority of the Bible from today's Christian perspective. It is this same perspective shift that is now needed when reading the account of creation in Genesis. Reading it as a simple explanation rather than a precise scientific text gives these verses a new perspective on creation.

Starting at the beginning of creation we see God as the creator of all things.

Genesis 1:1 (KJV)
1 In the beginning God created the heaven and the earth.

This is not the beginning of the story though. For God has no beginning, nor will he have an end. The Bible tells us God has always existed, leaving plenty of planning time before he created the universe and everything in it. The pre-creation time is explained by the following verses.

Psalm 90:2 (ERV)
2 You were God before the mountains were born, before the earth and the world were made. You have always been and will always be God!

We are also told that God was not alone but was accompanied by the Word who was also God.

John 1:1-2 (GNT)
The Word of Life

1 In the beginning the Word already existed; the Word was with God, and the Word was God.
2 From the very beginning the Word was with God.

The Holy Ghost is also a part of God. This makes the nature of God more complicated than that of mankind, making it difficult to explain as a physical human analogy will never by completely satisfying. The best one Christianity has been able to come up with is that God is three in one. All aspects of God should be revered, whether we fully understand them or not.

Luke 12:10 (ICB)
10 If a person says something against the Son of Man, he can be forgiven. But a person who says bad things against the Holy Spirit will not be forgiven.

At some point in time God created spirit beings. They were shouting for joy when the earth was created. These events took place chronologically before the creation accounts found in Genesis.

Job 38:4-7 (ERV)
4 "Where were you when I made the earth? If you are so smart, answer me.

5 And who decided how big the earth should be?
Who measured it with a measuring line?
6 What is the earth resting on? Who put the first
stone in its place
7 when the morning stars sang together and the
angels shouted with joy?

God lets these spirit beings choose their own
destiny, some of them chose well, others decided to
rebel against God. There was a battle in heaven and
one third of the Angels followed Satan and were
cast out of heaven.

Revelation 12:7-9 (TLB)
7 Then there was war in heaven; Michael and the
angels under his command fought the Dragon and
his hosts of fallen angels. 8 And the Dragon lost the
battle and was forced from heaven. 9 This great
Dragon—the ancient serpent called the devil, or
Satan, the one deceiving the whole world—was
thrown down onto the earth with all his army.

Jesus tells us that he saw Satan fall to the
earth. He was present, as the Word, when this
heavenly war took place.

Luke 10:17-18 (GNT)

17 The seventy-two men came back in great joy. "Lord," they said, "even the demons obeyed us when we gave them a command in your name!" 18 Jesus answered them, "I saw Satan fall like lightning from heaven.

All of these events took place before Adam and Eve were created in the Garden of Eden. There is a large time gap between Genesis 1:1 and Genesis 1:2. This is why we read that the world is without form and void in verse 2. Hardly a picture of splendour worthy of singing about and shouting for joy over as the Angels did at the earth's inception in Job 38:7.

Verse 2 describes the earth is a dark foreboding place, devastated by war from its original grandeur. The footnotes in The Living Bible support this point of view.

Genesis 1:2 (TLB)
2 the earth was[a] a shapeless, chaotic mass,* with the Spirit of God brooding over the dark vapours.*
Footnotes:

a.   Genesis 1:2 the earth was, or "the earth became." a shapeless, chaotic mass, or "shapeless and void." over the dark vapours, or "over the cloud of darkness," or "over the darkness and waters," or "over the dark gaseous mass." There is not one correct way to translate these words.

The creation accounts found in Genesis would be more accurately understood as re-creation accounts, or the renewing of the earth after being destroyed by a great battle. The description of these re-creation accounts are given from the perspective of being on the earth as they happen in a flowing story. First there is a glimmer of light, then the atmosphere clears and there is a divide in the waters.

Genesis 1:3-8 (NLV)
3 Then God said, "Let there be light," and there was light. 4 God saw that the light was good. He divided the light from the darkness. 5 Then God called the light day, and He called the darkness night. There was evening and there was morning, one day.
6 Then God said, "Let there be an open space between the waters. Let it divide waters from waters." 7 God made the open space, and divided the waters under the open space from the waters above the open space. And it was so. 8 Then God

called the open space Heaven. There was evening and there was morning, the second day.

Next the water separates and dry land appears. Plants start to flourish and cover the bare earth.

Genesis 1:9-13 (NLV)
9 Then God said, "Let the waters under the heavens be gathered into one place. Let the dry land be seen." And it was so. 10 Then God called the dry land Earth. He called the gathering of the waters Seas. And God saw that it was good. 11 Then God said, "Let plants grow from the earth, plants that have seeds. Let fruit trees grow on the earth that bring their kind of fruit with their own seeds." And it was so. 12 Plants grew out of the earth, giving their own kind of seeds. Trees grew with their fruit, and their kind of seeds. And God saw that it was good. 13 There was evening and there was morning, the third day.

Now the atmosphere is sufficiently clear to see the sun and the stars. Having light and dark from the first day would have required the sun to be shining on the earth from the beginning, but it is not until now that the atmosphere has cleared sufficiently for the sun, moon and stars to become fully visible from an earthly perspective.

Genesis 1:14-19 (NLV)
14 Then God said, "Let there be lights in the open space of the heavens to divide day from night. Let them tell the days and years and times of the year. 15 Let them be lights in the open space of the heavens to give light on the earth." And it was so. 16 Then God made the two great lights, the brighter light to rule the day, and the smaller light to rule the night. He made the stars also. 17 God put them in the open space of the heavens to give light on the earth, 18 to rule the day and the night. He divided the light from the darkness. And God saw that it was good. 19 There was evening and there was morning, the fourth day.

Creation is now focused on the fauna of the world culminating with land animals and mankind being created on day six.

Genesis 1:20-31 (NLV)
20 Then God said, "Let the waters be full of living things. Let birds fly above the earth in the open space of the heavens." 21 God made the big animals that live in the sea, and every living thing that moves through the waters by its kind, and every winged bird after its kind. And God saw that it was good. 22 God wanted good to come to them, saying, "Give birth to many. Grow in number. Fill

the waters in the seas. Let birds grow in number on the earth." 23 There was evening and there was morning, the fifth day.

24 Then God said, "Let the earth bring into being living things after their kind: Cattle and things that move upon the ground, and wild animals of the earth after their kind." And it was so. 25 Then God made the wild animals of the earth after their kind, and the cattle after their kind, and every thing that moves upon the ground after its kind. And God saw that it was good.

26 Then God said, "Let Us make man like Us and let him be head over the fish of the sea, and over the birds of the air, and over the cattle, and over all the earth, and over every thing that moves on the ground." 27 And God made man in His own likeness. In the likeness of God He made him. He made both male and female. 28 And God wanted good to come to them, saying, "Give birth to many. Grow in number. Fill the earth and rule over it. Rule over the fish of the sea, over the birds of the sky, and over every living thing that moves on the earth." 29 Then God said, "See, I have given you every plant that gives seeds that is on the earth, and every tree that has fruit that gives seeds. They will be food for you. 30 I have given every green plant for food to every animal of the earth, and to every bird of the sky, and to every thing that moves on the earth that has life." And it was so. 31 God saw

all that He had made and it was very good. There was evening and there was morning, the sixth day.

These six days of creation tell us about the steps in our world's creation process. Was this the first time the earth had life? The Bible is silent about any other periods of life on the earth, just as it is silent on the workings of our solar system. What method God used for his creation process can be debated along with how many cycles, or times of re-creating there may have been.

The exasperation Richard Dawkins has with young earth creationists may be justified. As he states in his interview, he is interested in the truth. He is interested in facts that can be scientifically proven. As I have stated, finding the truth is normally somewhere between the extremes.

Here is one fact, where science supports what the Bible has to say. The science behind the Big Bang theory teaches us the universe has been expanding and growing ever since the boom that started the whole process. Scientists speculate that this expansion will never end and it will continue to grow new solar systems indefinitely. This supports what the Bible tells us in:

Luke 1:32-33 NIV.

32 He will be great and will be called the Son of the Most High. The Lord God will give him the throne of his father David, 33 and he will reign over Jacob's descendants forever; his kingdom will never end."

And again in:

Isaiah 9:7 ICB
7 Power and peace will be in his kingdom. It will continue to grow. He will rule as king on David's throne and over David's kingdom. He will make it strong, by ruling with goodness and fair judgement. He will rule it forever and ever. The Lord of heaven's armies will do this because of his strong love for his people.

Bible scholars may not agree with this perspective for these scriptures, but then it was Bible scholars who didn't agree with Galileo. The scientific facts Galileo supported also required a new perspective on well-known Bible scripture.

The fact is, the Bible is not a scientific text book on how the world around us works. It is a book of Godly wisdom given to humanity, intended to reveal practical guidance on how to live now in this life and how to gain life everlasting.

The Bible may not reveal the time of our earth's beginnings but it does reveal to us who was there doing the creating. The scientific method of discovery is very good at gaining knowledge on how the physical world around us works. It deals with the tangible, quantitative, qualities of our world.

Through hypothesis and reproducible experimentation the scientific method has led mankind into many discoveries. Staying true to these scientific values is not possible when exploring the point before the Big Bang or creation occurred, a time before there was anything. At this pre-creation point there is nothing to measure, no physical properties to study or experiment with. Even forces such as gravity, magnetism or electromagnetism, no weak force, or strong interaction is present at this point. It is a time of nothing, not even a vacuum exists in the void, as there is no void. To have a void implies there is a gap between objects, objects that have not yet been brought into existence.

The downfall for the evolutionist is the fundamental principles of the scientific method. Proving how our physical world works through reproducible experimentation, is at the heart of science. Having no physical properties or

phenomena to work with at the time prior to the
Big Bang or creation, the scientific method is
helpless to explain
scientifically how the Big Bang boomed.

Theorizing the energy used for creation came
from inside the vacuum of nothingness misses the
meaning of nothingness. Nothingness is a time
where there was no vacuum or mysterious energy.
There was nothing. Evolutionists are left in the
uncomfortable position of explaining how
something, the universe, came from the nothing of
the pre-Big Bang era.

Pre-Big Bang is a spiritual time, a time that
can only be understood from a spiritual perspective.
For this understanding we need to get our
perspective from a spiritual source. No amount of
hypothesizing or experimentation will help us find
this kind of truth. As a Biblist I take my spiritual
guidance from the Bible, others might use different
sources they find more relevant.

The scientific method can unlock many
mysteries, but it is limited to the material workings
of things surrounding us. Some are hard to find or
understand, like nutrienos and dark matter.
Unlocking the mysterious workings of the
universe's beginning does not replace God as

creator, it only magnifies the need for his spiritual creativity before creation or the Big Bang took place.

To become educated in spiritual truths all we need to do, as Professor Dawkins has pointed out, is go away and read a book. May I suggest the Bible, when you read it like a Biblist, it has much wisdom to offer.

ABOUT THE AUTHOR

Clayton Carlson is a published freelance author within the Christian genre. He writes articles and bible studies for the Biblists.com web site, and has audio books and articles appearing on various podcast websites.

As a Biblist in the Berean tradition, at *biblists.com* Clayton Carlson shares biblical truths and studies the Bible to fully understand scripture by reviewing original texts of ancient believers while exploring modern theology.

Connect with Clayton B Carlson

I really appreciate you reading my book!

Find me on Facebook:
https://www.facebook.com/biblists/
Visit my website: www.Biblists.com

Other books by Clayton B Carlson

Biblist Apologetics
My Baby Died. Where is My Baby?
Searching For Immortality
The Eden Conspiracy
Thy Kingdom Come, The Next Big Thing.

www.ingramcontent.com/pod-product-compliance
Lightning Source LLC
Chambersburg PA
CBHW060632030426
42337CB00018B/3321